COLORING THE SHADES of Grief and Healing

A Teen/Young Adult Coloring Book
To Help Heal Through Grief

by Authors
Lyn Ragan and Dorothy Pigue

Coloring The Shades of Grief and Healing
Copyright © 2016 by Lyn Ragan and Dorothy Pigue

No part of this book shall be reproduced or transmitted in any form or by any means, electronic, mechanical, magnetic, photographic including photocopying, recording or by any information storage and retrieval system, without prior written permission of Lyn Ragan and Dorothy Pigue, except in the case of brief quotations embodied in critical articles and reviews.

No patent liability is assumed with respect to the use of the information contained herein. Although every precaution has been taken in the preparation of this book, the publisher and author assume no responsibility for errors or omissions. Neither is any liability assumed for damages resulting from the use of the information contained herein.

Cover and Book Design by *Lyn M Oney*
Illustrations © Lyn Ragan and Dorothy Pigue
Trade paper ISBN 978-0-9860205-0-6

Any Internet references contained in the work are current at publication time, but the authors cannot guarantee that a specific location will continue to be maintained.

To our Loved Ones in Heaven,
With Love and Grace...

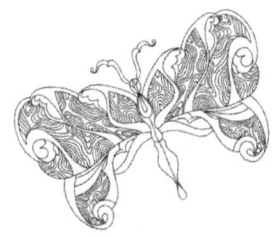

Other Books by Lyn Ragan

Wake Me Up! a true story
How Chip's Afterlife Saved Me
fb/wakemeupbook

We Need To Talk
Living With The Afterlife
fb/weneedtotalkbook

Signs From The Afterlife
Identifying Gifts From The Other Side
fb/signsfromtheafterlife

Signs From Pets In The Afterlife
Identifying Messages From Pets In Heaven
fb/signsfrompetsintheafterlife

Introduction

Lyn Ragan lost the *love of her life* in 2008. One second they were chatting on the phone and in the next, he was killed while preparing for work.

Her grief spiraled into a web of sadness she found difficult to break free of. All of their future dreams destroyed and her life altered forever, Lyn was taken by surprise when she started receiving communications from her deceased fiancé— via dreams. Ms. Ragan would later write about their visits and eventually publish several books on the subject of *Afterlife Communications*.

Her mission in life is to help those who grieve from the loss of a loved one; her ultimate goal to replace painful grief with belief and understanding. Lyn works tirelessly helping those she can reach to understand this physical life is not the end of who we are, and that love and life lives forever— as do our Souls.

Dorothy Pigue was born into a family of clairvoyants. As a young child, she began hearing the voices of spirits around her. It took many years for Dorothy to realize she could communicate with the spirit world and with loved ones who have crossed over. Wanting to enhance her gifts and psychic abilities, she trained with Carl Woodall at the *Atlanta Metaphysical Center* in Atlanta, Georgia, and became a graduate of *The Anastasi System of Psychic Development* in 2014.

Dorothy is also a Master Herbalist who has been practicing as a Korean Medicine Woman since 1996. She is a Clinical Certified Hypnotherapist, a Certified Usui/Holy Fire Reiki ® Practitioner, and an author.

Dorothy's mission in life is to share her gifts and abilities in hopes of removing the *pain of grief*. Healing begins with love and from the other side, *Love* is the message she enjoys sharing.

Authors Lyn Ragan and Dorothy Pigue are excited to come together on a personal undertaking to help bring peace, love, and healing into the hearts of those who grieve.

Our Wish For You…

Every journey that winds through grief is different. No two paths are the same. Your thoughts and your feelings are very unique to you. It is so important to take the time to "breathe", and coloring can give you that space to be still with your deepest inner thoughts.

Our wish is to help you cope with your loss and receive *healing* at the same time. That is why we produced this coloring book. Each page has a descriptive word or phrase attached to it. They are as follows:

loss; initial shock; disbelief; absence; pain; emptiness; isolation; breathe; one day at a time; baby steps; be gentle with yourself; surviving loss; grief is individual; no rule books; rest your mind; acceptance; hope-faith-love; healing; make a wish; always missing you; finding peace; memories of you; new beginnings; life is different now; I love you; I miss you; compassion; transformation; my spirit; my soul; living again; love lives forever.

From our personal experiences, we believe each one of these statements is a dynamic blueprint toward loss, acceptance, and in time, healing.

As you start to color a particular page, focus on its affirmation and ask how it makes you feel. Ask what the words mean to you, what the emotions did or are doing to you. Allow each letter you color, and each sensation you witness, to release from your being and your body. To begin to survive your loss, and your grief, is to acknowledge the pain that resides within you.

Our hope is that these coloring pages will help to heal your broken spirit. Remember— there is no time limit for your grief and there are no rule books either. Take all the time you need.

One step, one day, and one coloring page… at a time.

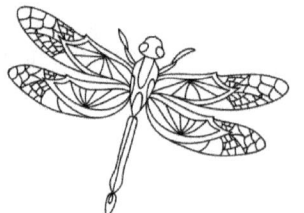

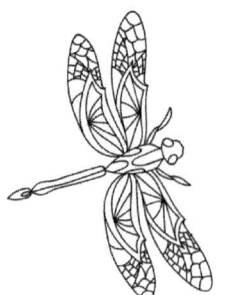

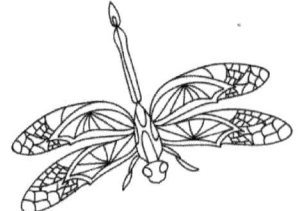

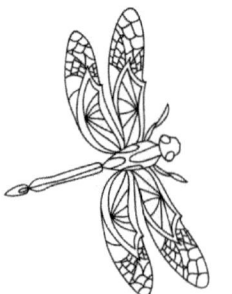

www.ingramcontent.com/pod-product-compliance
Lightning Source LLC
LaVergne TN
LVHW081400060426
835510LV00016B/1911